AN ANALYTICAL SURVEY OF THE FIFTEEN TWO-PART INVENTIONS BY J.S. BACH

Theodore O. Johnson

UNIVERSITY PRESS OF AMERICA

LANHAM • NEW YORK • LONDON

Copyright © 1982 by

University Press of America,™ Inc.

4720 Boston Way
Lanham, MD 20706

3 Henrietta Street
London WC2E 8LU England

Library of Congress Cataloging in Publication Data

Johnson, Theodore O.
 An analytical survey of the fifteen two-part inventions
by J.S. Bach.

 Includes index.
 1. Bach, Johann Sebastian, 1685–1750. Inventions,
harpsichord, BWV 772-786. I. Title.
MT145.B14J58   1982   786.1'092'4   81–43826
ISBN 0–8191–2582–2
ISBN 0–8191–2583–0 (pbk.)

TO CAROL

CONTENTS

PREFACE

The fifteen *Two-Part Inventions* were composed as pedagogical pieces during the period from 1720 to 1723, while Bach was living in Cöthen, and they remain, today, essential to any complete and proper study of the keyboard. As individual pieces having mostly just two voice-parts, and being arranged (somewhat differently from the order in which they were originally composed) in such a way as to utilize--in ascending order by pitch, starting with C--only certain major and minor keys which employ no more than four sharps and four flats, they provide instruction which, although demanding, requires less performance facility than that required by the pieces of the *Well-Tempered Clavier*, each volume of which explores multi-voice writing involving both preludes and fugues, also in ascending order by pitch, but with pieces in major and minor keys on each of the twelve tones.

Because they represent a unique and magnificent body of literature, encompassing many contrapuntal and other musical devices which exhibit remarkable economy of material within concise forms constantly capable of offering new twists to fascinate the mind and refresh the musical spirit, the *Inventions* are valuable to students of Eighteenth-Century counterpoint as well as to pianists at various levels of achievement. This study, therefore, is intended for supplemental use by piano students and counterpoint students to help guide them along the structural paths Bach took when he created the *Inventions*.

The key arrangement of the *Inventions* is: (1) C Major (no sharps or flats); (2) C Minor (three flats); (3) D Major (two sharps); (4) D Minor (one flat); (5) Eb Major (three flats); (6) E Major (four sharps); (7) E Minor (one sharp); (8) F Major (one flat); (9) F Minor (four flats); (10) G Major (one sharp); (11) G Minor (two flats); (12) A Major (three sharps); (13) A Minor (no sharps or flats); (14) Bb Major (two flats); and (15) B Minor (two sharps). Thus inventions based on all the major keys having up to three flats and four sharps, and all the minor keys having up to four flats and two sharps, are included (minor-key inventions on all the white keys, and major-key inventions on two black keys--Eb and Bb--in addition to all the white keys except for B).

Certain of the *Two-Part Inventions* are based on very brief melodic ideas, termed motives, and others, on broader ideas termed subjects. Numbers One, Four, Seven, Eight, Ten, and Thirteen were the first composed,[1] and these inventions (in C major and all its closely related keys) generally employ short generating ideas, whereas the remainder employ longer ones (although Numbers Three and Four have ideas of approximately the same length). A contrapuntal accompaniment to the opening idea is found in nine of the fifteen *Inventions*.

Imitation is one of the most important devices of the *Inventions*, all of which begin with the motive or subject in the treble and continue with its restatement in the bass. Two-thirds make use of imitation at the lower octave (or in one case the double octave), and the remainder, imitation at the fifth (lower eleventh), employing both the tonal answer and the real answer. Imitation sometimes goes beyond the boundaries of the opening idea, at least to some extent, and in two instances (Inventions Two and Eight) involves sufficient length to be called canon.

Other devices which play a prominent role are sequence, melodic inversion, and invertible counterpoint. The latter is sometimes applied on a large structural scale, with entire sections based upon previous sections having the two voice-parts exchanged, and at other times on a much smaller scale involving perhaps one- or two-bar passages--either adjacent or separated by intervening material.

Most of the *Inventions* are sectional in nature with sections defined either by conclusive-sounding cadences or by recurrence of material which has been modified through transposition and other means; however,

---

[1]Hans T. David and Arthur Mendel, *The Bach Reader* (New York: W.W. Norton & Company, 1966), p. 38.

continuity is consistently maintained through elision or rhythmic activity which persists from the end of one section into the beginning of another. All are characterized by motivic or thematic unity in conjunction with tonal and contrapuntal variety, and change of tonality is one of the principal means by which contrast is achieved, for the subject or motive frequently shows up intact, within a different (but closely related) key, sometimes transposed to different scale degrees within that key.

Each of the individual analyses which follows has been limited to a discussion of what I consider to be the *most* important features of structure, melody, harmony, and rhythm. The student is encouraged to use each analysis as a point-of-departure for further investigation into the many fascinating details which abound throughout the *Inventions*.

April 1982   Theodore O. Johnson

                          East Lansing, Michigan

CHAPTER 1:   INVENTION NUMBER ONE (C MAJOR)

This invention is divided into three sections, each ending with a conclusive cadence (measures 6-7, 14-15, and 21-22).   Its germ idea is the short subject or motive which appears first in the treble (a procedure common to all Bach's *Two-Part Inventions*), unaccompanied (a less unique feature of the *Inventions*), and is then imitated by the bass at the lower octave, all within the first measure. Measure 2, in effect, answers these statements with a transposition at the dominant.

Example 1:   Measures 1-3

The opening motive is then inverted in the treble, as the first stage of a sequence, which descends through three more stages, while the lower voice presents a transposed version of the first four notes of the motive in augmentation--sequentially too, but with one less stage.   A modulation to the dominant major key--the opening key of the forthcoming second section--occurs about half-way through section one (Example 2).

The concluding portion of section one has the original motive on different scale degrees within the key of G major, in the bass, followed in the treble by its inversion, the last half of which continues sequentially and leads into a perfect authentic cadence (Example 3).

Example 2.   Measures 3-5

Example 3.   Measures 5-7

   Section two generally tends to parallel section one
in invertible counterpoint, manifested by various intervals of inversion.   Measures 7 and 8, for example,
illustrate this exchange somewhat freely between the
treble and bass from the first two measures of the invention.

Example 4.   Measures 7-9

   A two-measure passage, mostly in C major, intrudes
upon this pattern, however, when the inverted motive
(with an attached eighth-note figure in the bass similar to that found in the treble during measure 1)
is treated sequentially in each voice, the upper imitating the lower at the fifth (Example 5).   A modulation to D minor at the end of measure 10 sets the stage

Example 5. Measures 9-11

for a resumption of the invertible counterpoint in measure 11, and for two and one-half measures from this
point, the passage from measures 3ff is paralleled, e-
ven to the extent of modulating the same distance (here
from D minor to A minor) at the corresponding location
(exploiting a cross relation, as it does). Actually,
the bass line here remains strict with the treble line
from before, almost to the end of the section.

Example 6. Measures 11-15

    Section three begins more-or-less transitional-
ly--as does the final section in certain other inven-
tions--with an extended pattern in the treble consist-
ing of first the inverted motive followed by a sustained note, then the original form, likewise followed
by a sustained note. This, as a two-measure unit, comprises the first stage of a sequence which is then
taken through another stage. The bass begins by imitating this configuration at the fifth (lower eleventh),

and ends by imitating at the fourth (lower twelfth) because of an intervallic adjustment in the middle of measure 16. It too is treated sequentially. The tonal result of this activity is a series of transient modulations leading away from the relative minor key, back to the tonic, through D minor; however, measure 18, the last measure involved in this pattern, overshoots the tonic key, temporarily emphasizing F major, before C major is firmly re-established in measure 20.

Example 7. Measures 15-19

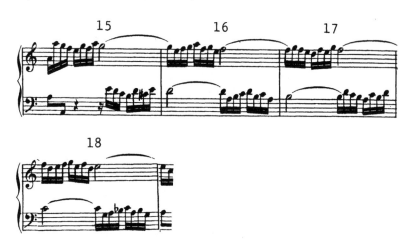

A passage based on inverted melodic material from measures 3f (and 11f, in invertible counterpoint) ensues, followed in turn by separate statements of the motive, right-side-up in the bass, and upside-down in the treble. Before a final bass entry can complete itself, the piece comes to an end.

Example 8. Measures 19-22

CHAPTER 2:   INVENTION NUMBER TWO (C MINOR)

Like the more famous Invention in F Major, this one
in C Minor is atypical in its opening imitative procedures, because it employs a canon--which remains strict,
at the octave, to the beginning of measure 11. Although
this device tends to cloud the issue of what comprises
the germinal idea, the treble portion extending to the
beginning of measure 3 is fairly well defined as a subject by the cadential figure which has been built into
its melodic line.

Example 9.   Measures 1-3

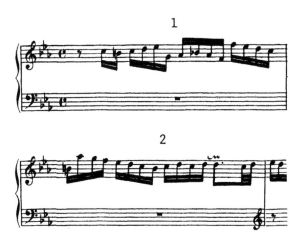

A countersubject, of sorts, appears in the treble
during measures 3-4, as a continuation of the canon's
antecedent voice, and although it is found completely
intact along with the subject at only one other point
in the invention (measures 13-14) outside the opening

section, fragments abound elsewhere, and of course the canonical procedure ensures its reappearance in the bass during measures 5-6, along with motives from the subject, but not the subject, itself, as an episodic passage gets under way. The traditional key change away from the tonic, in this case to the relative major, is accomplished just as the second voice is completing its imitation of the subject portion of the canon--rather early within the section, in fact.

Example 10. Measures 3-7

Eb major prevails then throughout all the rest of section one, as the canon unfolds with material which is sometimes freely, and sometimes strictly, derived from the opening subject.

Example 11. Measures 7-11

No striking cadence appears at measures 10-11, but the format for section two, which resembles that of the first invention, involves a reiteration of section one in invertible counterpoint (minus an interrupting passage such as the one in the previous invention). A subtly deferred modulation to the dominant minor key results in a slightly modified beginning to the bass statement, which--as the treble temporarily continues to supply stylistically similar new material--leads off a new canon, in measures 11ff, on the same material employed by the old canon. The subject portion of this statement continues within G minor, and its imitation in the treble, along with accompanying counterpoint (measures 13-14), follows the pattern set in measures 3-4 by providing a modulation up a third, here to Bb major (the subtonic major key), near the end of measure 14. The canonical imitation concludes at precisely the same location within section two (the beginning of measure 21) that its original version did within section one.

Example 12.   Measures 11-21

As the treble ceases its canonical imitation of the bass at the octave with a two-measure time interval, the bass (measure 21) begins imitating the treble (from measure 20) at the sixth (lower tenth), with a one-measure time interval. Its material--which was first found in its present form during measure 8 in the treble--is based upon the opening two-note figure of the piece, followed by running sixteenth notes, and it reappears in the treble one final time, modulating to C minor in measure 22 and leading to a final pair of subjects in the original key in measures 23-24 (treble) and 25-26 (bass), accompanied by countersubject fragments. The latter statement becomes free in the penultimate measure in order to set up the conclusion of the piece.

Example 13. Measures 21-27

CHAPTER 3:   INVENTION NUMBER THREE (D MAJOR)

A larger number of sections than are found in Inventions One and Two, results--in the D-Major Inven-
tion--from a more abundant use of well-defined cadences
(measures 11-12, 23-24, 37-38, and 58-59), and all of
these cadences exploit similar rhythmic and, to some
extent, melodic and harmonic formulas. The opening subject, hovering as it does about the tonic triad, is
custom-made for the type of pedal treatment it receives
later on. It has distinct motives which bear a curious
resemblance to each other--the first part of measure
2's motive growing out of the last part of measure
1's--and these ideas (especially the first) are later
isolated for separate treatment. The initial upbeat
seems to have independent importance too, when it is
metrically displaced over to the first beat in the bass
during cadential patterns and also when it is subse-
quently enlarged to encompass most of a measure (for
example, measures 12, 14, etc.). Like the first two
inventions, this one has a subject which is unaccompanied from the start, and the treble is imitated at the
lower octave by the bass, which in this case overlaps
slightly with the treble, as the treble finishes the
subject.

Example 14.   Measures 1-5

Following these relatively standard opening procedures, an episode is initiated by the subject's first

motive (from measure 1), which appears transposed, and
in two different versions (measures 5 and 6), preceded
by upbeat material and accompanied by a broken-octave
dominant pedal, which pivots and becomes a tonic pedal.
A rare moment of literal repetition in measures 7-8
then precedes the same motive in its original form but
on still different staff degrees in the treble (measure
9) and bass (measure 10), following which a perfect
authentic cadence concludes the section in A major.

Example 15. Measures 5-12

This cadence, like most interior cadences in Bach's
Two-Part Inventions, is harmonically conclusive, but
rhythmically continuous. The sixteenth notes (measure
12), which provide continuity by prefixing the original
upbeat material, create an additional upbeat motive on-
to which motive one is then attached (measure 13) to
form a unit that is given more attention from here on,
than is the original subject. This unit--followed by a
portion of the broken-octave pattern first heard in
measure 5--appears first in the bass (measures 12-14)
and is imitated at the fifth by the treble (measures
14-16), but not before the treble, in turn, has been
prefixed by a rising-fourth, eighth-note idea, which
shows up again in both the bass (measure 15) and treble
(measure 17). Invertible counterpoint between the second section's beginning and that of the first section
does not play a role here, as it did in the first two
inventions, but it is used internally within section
two, for example at measures 15-16, on the material

from 13-14. A modulation into B minor (through E minor) takes place during this passage.

Example 16. Measures 12-18

Sequence has a part in spinning out section two into the B-minor cadence at measures 23-24. Three descending stages are used with motive one at measures 19-21 in the treble, accompanied by a sequence of fewer stages in the bass, followed by an inverted presentation of the enlarged upbeat material from measure 12 (at 21), and then motive one, itself.

Example 17. Measures 19-24

The first part of section three is also based on sequence, with the treble having two large four-measure stages, and the bass imitating the treble, freely, beginning at measure 26. The two-measure union of ideas from 12-13 contributes the material for the first half of each stage, with a sustained note occupying the second half. A modulation into D major (through E minor) early within the passage generates direction and relates to a change in the interval of imitation at measure 28. As this chain of events concludes without the bass material ever fulfilling itself sequentially, another modulation takes place back to A major (31-32).

Example 18. Measures 24-32

At measures 33-34, most of the original subject is given out in *durchbrochene Arbeit* fashion, motive one being located in the treble, followed by motive two, in the bass down two octaves. Motive two is also stated by the bass in conjunction with motive one by the treble in measure 33, but with its tail upside-down. The principal material of measures 35 and 36 is motive one, respectively in the treble and bass, and the cadence at 37-38 anticipates the exact melodic formula of the final cadence, as it confirms the rhythmic-harmonic scheme of both previous cadences.

Example 19. Measures 33-38

The transitional nature of section four's beginning is reminiscent of that in the final section of Invention One. The very first measure (38) pivots back
to the tonic key and--along with the following mea-
sure--reinstates, in transposition, the bass material
from measures 12-13, the beginning of section two. The
last half of this idea (motive one) sets off a three-
stage sequence in the bass (measures 39-41), the last
stage being mostly doubled at the upper sixth (plus an
octave) by the treble, following which the first half
is presented upside-down (measure 42) in preparation for
the return.

Example 20.   Measures 38-42

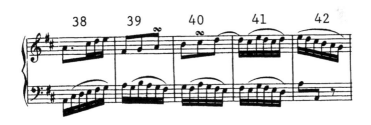

Except for an inverted upbeat, the return is ver-
batim with the beginning for several measures; however,
at the distinctive broken-octave pedal passage (47-50),
the two voices appear in invertible counterpoint with
each other from the earlier passage (5-8), and at the
tonic, rather than the dominant, for the conclusion of
the piece is not far off. Motive one then resumes in
the treble (51) and continues imitatively in the bass
(52) just prior to a deceptive cadence (53-54) which
defines the beginning of a coda.

Example 21.   Measures 43-54

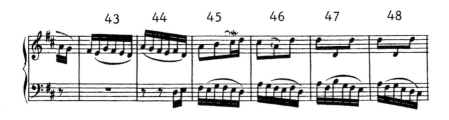

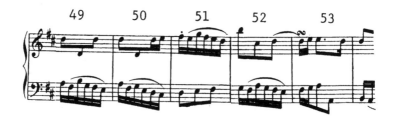

The coda begins by bringing back material from measures 13ff, down a ninth, most faithfully in the treble, but temporarily in the bass too. The treble's third bar (56) ends the relationship, however, and begins a new one with the passage at 35ff, down a fifth. After one measure, the bass follows suit, and the work concludes with a transposition of measures 36-38.

Example 22. Measures 54-59

CHAPTER 4:   INVENTION NUMBER FOUR (D MINOR)

A two-measure subject gets the D-Minor Invention
under way, establishing a pattern of harmonic rhythm
which remains constant throughout the piece, except at
or near cadence points, with one chord change per measure. Statements appear at measures 1-2 in the treble,
3-4 in the bass, at the lower octave, and 5-6 in the
treble again, but at the upper octave. The first statement is unaccompanied, while the second and third statements employ free invertible counterpoint involving similar eighth-note patterns. The high treble statement
at measures 5-6 is, from its second note, continued sequentially at 7-8, where the bass begins a sequence
too, and 9-10, with both voices displaying a type of
momentum which makes modulation--here, into the relative major key--seem inevitable.

Example 23.   Measures 1- 11

As section one progresses at measure 11, the bass takes over the slightly paraphrased account of the subject which the treble has just been using, as the treble introduces another derivative thought involving half-bar repeated groupings. These two ideas are likewise used in sequence (measures 11-12 and 13-14), following which the bass adheres to its scheme for two more measures--with a different interval of restatement--as the treble becomes free and then responds with an inversion of the subject's opening measure. Section one ends with a perfect authentic cadence, at measures 17-18.

Example 24. Measures 11-18

Section two goes along with the precedent established in earlier inventions by setting out with a bass statement of the subject (measures 18-19) in the new key, F major. The treble supports this statement with a dominant pedal, but is denied the traditional opportunity to imitate, by the bass, which sequences the entire subject (20-21). Measures 22-25 re-examine the passage from 11-14 but with modified treble material in the bass, and bass material freely inverted in the treble (Example 25).

A new upper-voice transposition of the subject (26-27) in the dominant minor key is followed by a somewhat free measure of sixteenths (28), and then a dominant pedal in A minor enters in the bass to set up--one measure prematurely--a passage, at 30-33, similar to the earlier one at 18-21, but with the voices exchanged

20   *Chapter 4*

Example 25. Measures 18-25

in invertible counterpoint. Here, however, the sixteenths begin on the third scale degree, as opposed to
the first, before, providing an element of contrast
heightened by subtle modifications of the line, which
results in a constantly shifting interval of inversion.
The treble gets out a free third sequential stage at
measures 34-35, as the bass pedal ceases, and the section starts drawing to a close.

Example 26. Measures 26-38

Invention Number Four   21

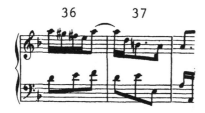

A tonally unstable passage gets section three under way with modified statements of the subject by the bass in G minor (measures 38-39), treble in F major (40-41), and bass again, modulating back to D minor (42-43). Extensive root movement by descending fifth (measures 38-42) nourishes the transitional character of this passage, which stabilizes with the return. Measures 44-45 initiate this return, by bringing back 5-6, after which 46-47 resurrect the bass part from 3-4. Following a deceptive cadence at 48-49, a brief coda, the principal thematic feature of which is the freely inverted subject (49-50), closes the invention.

Example 27. Measures 38-52

CHAPTER 5: INVENTION NUMBER FIVE (Eb MAJOR)

Several procedures of Invention Five offer contrast to those of the preceding inventions, the most
immediately noticeable being the use cf two voices from
the beginning--a feature of nine of the *Two-Part Inventions*, but none of the first four. The second voice
carries a countersubject along with the first entry of
the subject, a circumstance which is frequently taken
advantage of in inventions having subjects which are
accompanied from the beginning. The substantial length
of this subject dwarfs the germinal ideas of Inventions
One, Three, and Four, although it never really becomes
canonical, like the idea in Invention Two. The modulation to the dominant major key in measure 4--before the
subject has completed itself--also comprises something
new, which according to traditional principles, requires imitation *not* at the octave, as in the first four
inventions, but rather at the fifth, and imitation which
is tonal, as opposed to real, as well.

The subject begins with sequence, its head motive
from measure 1 being restated up one degree in the second measure. The third and fourth measures of the subject are integrated more by rhythmic, than by melodic
means. Much interest centers around the countersubject, which emerges in the bass during the last half
of measure 1, and which has three separate sixteenth-
note motives (each characterized by a changing-tone configuration) that are distributed differently at various locations throughout the piece. The countersubject's first motive, a predominantly broken-third idea,
is found at the end of measure 1, and sequenced at the
beginning of measure 2; its second motive appears at
the end of measure 2, and is freely repeated at the
beginning of 3; its third motive comes at the end of
measure 3, and is freely sequenced at the beginning of
4. The countersubject is then completed by a transposed reappearance of its second motive, which has the
responsibility for effecting a convincing modulation to

Bb major, since the subject is somewhat noncommittal in this regard.

Example 28.   Measures 1-5

     This second motive of the countersubject is taken over by the treble in imitation, at the beginning of measure 5, as the bass begins a tonal answer. Imitation by the treble here fills in the area corresponding to that occupied by the first two quarters of the bass in measure 1. The subject and countersubject together, in measures 5-8, provide invertible counterpoint with their counterparts in 1-4, each imitating the other at the fifth (or lower fourth, as the case may be) until about the middle of measure 8, where necessary tonal adjustments cause both to switch to the fourth (or lower fifth) as an interval of imitation in order to accommodate the modulation up a fourth from Bb major to Eb major, in response to the original modulation up a fifth, from Eb to Bb (Example 29).

     An episode of just three measures (9-11) rounds out section one, its brevity being necessitated by the sizable length of the subject and its answer. The episode is sequential, with each stage based upon the events of measure 5, in invertible counterpoint. The **treble pursues sequence on the subject's earliest mo-tive** one step further than it was taken in measures 5-6 (and 1-2), and the bass, utilizing an arrangement which consists of the countersubject's second motive,

Example 29. Measures 5-9

followed by its first (in imitation of the treble from measure 5--beyond the scope of the subject), follows suit, becoming slightly free, however--mostly due to displacement at the octave--during the last half of 11.

Example 30. Measures 9-12

In broad terms, section two (measures 12-23) parallels section one (1-12) in invertible counterpoint, in the manner of Inventions One and Two, but with certain alterations. Measure 15, for example, relates back to measure 8 rather than 4 in invertible counterpoint, because section two does not employ a subject-answer relationship like that of section one, but rather what might be called an answer-answer relationship, since both entries take the format of the tonal answer. The first entry--in the bass accompanied by the countersubject in the treble--begins with an immediate change into C, the relative minor, and then modulates up a fourth (rather than a fifth) to F minor (measures 12-15). Each voice then imitates the other strictly (16-19/12-15), as opposed to freely in section one (5-8/1-4), with the result that there is another modulation up a fourth, to Bb minor, a non closely related key.

Example 31. Measures 12-20

The episode in measures 20-22 obviously relates to the previous episode in 9-11, but it is treated differently. The subject's head motive formerly was used in the treble voice, moving sequentially upward; here, it appears in the bass, moving sequentially downward. In the earlier passage's bass, motives two and one of the countersubject were alternated; here, in the treble, only motive two is used, twice within each one-bar sequential stage, which, like each stage of the bass, moves in the opposite direction from before. As a consequence, the first part of each measure exploits invertible counterpoint with the first part of its respective counterpart from before, strictly, but the last part does so only freely. This episode modulates, through Ab major to F minor, and leads into a perfect authentic cadence at measures 22-23.

Example 32. Measures 20-23

The cadence sets up a false return (in Ab major) of the subject's opening two bars, in the treble (23-24), accompanied sequentially, in the bass, by motive one of the countersubject (now from the beginning), then motive two (during the latter part of 24). The subsequent two measures (25-26) freely invert the counterpoint of these two measures and bring back the tonic key. With the return, the first three bars of the subject and countersubject (measures 27-29) appear exactly as they did at the opening of the invention. The fourth bar (30), however, which has a sequential continuation of the third, extends the subject from within and serves to prevent the modulation associated with the original subject by pointing towards and tonicizing the subdominant, from which level the subject's ending at the tonic can parallel its original ending at the dominant, so the piece can come to a graceful conclusion without yet another answer. Measure 30, in fact, leads into 31 in exactly the same way that 3 led into 4, but transposed up a fourth in the treble (and down a fifth in the bass), and the subject then continues almost as if nothing unusual had taken place. Motive three of the countersubject, which has been slighted since its first appearance at measures 3-4, becomes paramount among the countersubject motives during and after this interior extension where it is taken through several stages of sequence in the bass before it gives in to motive two at the end of measure 31. Deferment of the conclusion until the middle of measure 32, two beats after the subject has ended, makes a perfect authentic cadence possible (Example 33).

Example 33.   Measures 23-32

CHAPTER 6:   INVENTION NUMBER SIX (E MAJOR)

Invertible counterpoint plays an important role in most of the *Two-Part Inventions*, but in no other invention does it exhibit an influence on the structure like that in Invention Six, where its pervasiveness at sections' beginnings establishes a more-or-less standard type of three-part form, with a statement (measures 1-20), digression (21-42), and restatement (43-62), the original statement being repeated by itself, and the digression (which provides tonal, but not thematic variety) and restatement, repeated together.

Again, as in Invention Five, both voices enter at the beginning, each voice with material manifesting an equality which is to be reinforced by constant contrapuntal association throughout the piece. The treble line may be logically construed as the subject (as in the other inventions), however, and the bass line as a countersubject moving largely in contrary motion. Most of the subject's first three measures comprise a descending head motive which is completely syncopated (all in eighth-notes or the equivalent), completely conjunct, slightly chromatic, and replete with suspensions, after which the fourth measure has a more active tail motive which exploits neighboring tones to embellish the arpeggiated tonic triad. These opening events then reappear with the two voices exchanged in invertible counterpoint during the next four measures (5-8), still in the tonic key.

Example 34.   Measures 1-9

The ensuing passage employs modified versions of subject and countersubject material, starting out with a modulation into the dominant major key, as the first stage of a two-stage sequence unfolds. This sequence (measures 9-10 and 11-12) is based, in the treble, on a telescoped, disjunct account of the subject's head motive, followed by a somewhat skeletonized version of the tail (melodically outlining a seventh chord rather than a triad, as originally), and in the bass, on an abbreviated, disjunct version of the countersubject. During the next three measures (13-15), head material from the subject wins out temporarily over tail material, in the treble, as the bass keeps its countersubject material, partially disjunct, and partially conjunct. For the remainder of this section, the subject's tail, in one form or another, is of prime motivic importance. It leads into a cadence at measures 17-18, following which it extends the final chord of that cadence into measure 20, dominating the bass as it does so, and also being suggested, in distilled form, in the treble.

Example 35. Measures 9-20

The first eight measures of section two (21-28)
bring back the opening eight measures of the invention,
in invertible counterpoint, within B major. The passage is almost, but not quite, strict, because the interval of inversion enlarges at measure 25, where the
treble part is displaced upward by two octaves in relationship to the bass part at measure 5.

Example 36. Measures 21-29

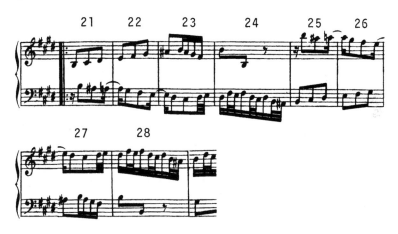

During the remaining portion of section two (measures 29-42), where most of the piece's modulatory activity is focused, the treble part is given over to the
subject's tail motive, interrupted by occasional head-
motive fragments, while the bass carries mostly even
eighth-notes, which--rhythmically, at least--make ref-
erence to the countersubject. In the treble, sequence,
both strict (beginning at the end of measure 28) and
free (measures 33ff), is used as an integrating device.
Sequence also shows up in the bass at measures 35-38.

The section ends with a perfect authentic cadence in G-sharp minor.

Example 37. Measures 29-42

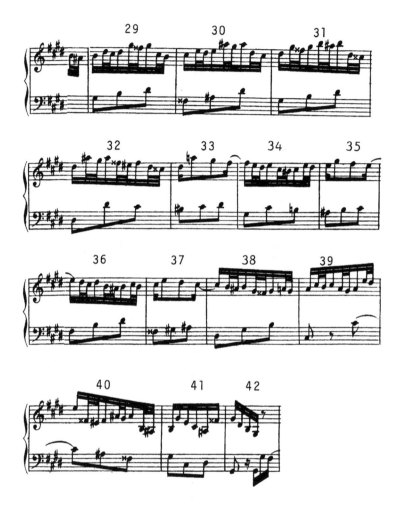

Section three, like section two, begins by restating the opening eight measures of the piece in invertible counterpoint, but in the tonic key, and with added twists contributed by the treble doubling (in compound tenths) of the tail motive at measure 46, and the bass doubling (in sixths) at 50. Its continuation, however, differs from that of section two, by remaining the same

with that of section one, still in invertible counterpoint, albeit free, for six more measures (51-56). Here
the bass remains strict with the treble from 9-14,
at the lower twelfth, while the treble restores the
earlier bass line, mostly at the upper fourth (eleventh), but also at the octave, for the beginning note
of alternate measures (51, 53, and 55). Transposition,
of course, is necessary for keeping this passage in E
major, for its counterpart at measures 9ff went off into B major. The bass at 57-58 confirms the treble from
15-16, after the invertible counterpoint ends, but octave displacement starts freeing the relationship in
58, and the final four measures of the invention con-
clude somewhat differently from the final four measures of section one, with the tail motive--which is
again predominant--ascending, rather than descending.

Example 38. Measures 43-62

CHAPTER 7:   INVENTION NUMBER SEVEN (E MINOR)

Invention Seven shares several features with Invention One, being approximately the same length, having the same number of sections, and using a half-bar
motive along with its imitation at the lower octave in
measure 1, followed by a transposition of both motive
and imitation to the dominant in measure 2. There is
even a slight resemblance between the motives of these
two pieces, although this one begins on the fifth scale
degree, rather than the first.

Example 39.   Measures 1-3

Measures 3-6 are basically episodic in nature despite the presence of the motive intact on several oc-
casions--a circumstance which often results from the
use of a short motive as the basis for a contrapuntal
work. At measure 3--as part of the first stage of a
sequence--the treble has been given first the motive
itself, then an inversion of beat four, measure 1,
and finally the first four notes of the motive transposed, while the bass uses the same materials it had
in measure 1, in the same order, but with transposition. Measure 4 then sequences measure 3, and confirms the chord from the end of 3 as a pivot chord
leading into the relative major key. During the first
half of measure 5, the bass takes over the material
found in the treble within the last half of measures 3
and 4, and sequences it, as the treble becomes somewhat free, with only implications of the original motive in its sixteenth-notes. The sequence continues

37

rhythmically, but not melodically, into measure 6, following which the harmonic rhythm accelerates for the cadence which concludes section one, at measures 6-7.

Example 40. Measures 3-7

In many inventions, section two gets under way with the two voices reversing roles from the beginning of section one, but here the treble once again leads the way, and then dwells on a trill, as the bass imitates freely--its first two notes being inverted--two octaves down. Then, instead of picking up on the trill to follow suit with the treble, the bass holds on to its version of the motive, in a freely sequential passage which leads to a progression--in the middle of measure 9--having certain features of a cadence, but coming off as less conclusive structurally because of its proximity to the earlier cadence at 6-7. Tonally, it points toward D major, but C-natural, which ensues, tends to reconfirm G major, temporarily. The treble brings in the motive at the end of measure 9 and then focuses on the configuration from beat four of measure 1 in various guises, as the bass again becomes freely sequential--on the motive, within the framework of consistent sixteenths--and modulates into B minor. Measures 11 and 12 provide contrapuntal convergence and tightening, as the end of section two approaches. The motive appears twice in the treble in measure 11 (during the middle of which there is a slight effect of half cadence). Premature imitation by the bass starting at the end of measure 11 creates stretto, a device

which for obvious reasons is rarely used in conjunction
with a motive this brief. Then, as the treble at the
beginning of measure 12 sequences itself from the end
of 11, further stretto results with the bass, which has
not yet finished the motive. A final entry of the motive in the bass, at the end of measure 12, has its
last beat sequenced at the beginning of 13, just before
the B-minor cadence which concludes section two.

Example 41. Measures 7-13

Section three begins transitionally, as do several
other concluding sections in the *Two-Part Inventions*.
The very first chord, in fact, is a pivot chord leading into A minor, which lasts for only a short time,
following which G major takes over, for not much longer, before E minor, the tonic key, returns at the end
of measure 14. With the beginning of section three, the
bass starts a sequence constructed on the opening motive prefixed by two notes, as the treble presents even
eighth-notes. The sequence dissipates in measure 15,

as only a one-beat fragment of the motive survives into a half cadence, which stands at approximately the
same location within section three that the cadence in
measure 9 stood within section two.

Example 42. Measures 13-15

Some semblance of return is apparent in the treble, starting with the last two notes of measure 15,
with melodic inversion occurring at the end of beat
one in 16, but the passage does not sound like a true
return because of instability, which is created by the
use of a dominant pedal, the raised seventh and sixth
scale degrees in a descending fashion, and melodic ap-
pendages, which--along with the motive--appear in half-
bar sequential stages, ending late in measure 17.

Example 43. Measures 16-17

The bass then abandons its pedal and proceeds to
imitate almost this entire treble line, while in the
treble, at measures 18-19, another sequence evolves,
this one based upon a submotive extracted from the al-
ready changed version found just previously, in 16-17.
This treble sequence also has half-bar stages, and it
ends near the middle of 19, just before the bass finishes its imitation, although a new, shorter sequence
emerges in the treble at the close of 19 (Example 44).

Example 44.   Measures 18-19

     Still more sequence is used by the bass, starting
in measure 20, and involving yet another enlarged-upon
version of the motive, but there are only two stages,
and the second stage becomes free before it can be completed. A bass statement of the motive commencing on
G during the first half of measure 21 generates further examination of the fragment comprising beat two,
on the third and fourth beats. A deceptive progression between measures 21 and 22 then initiates a two-
bar coda, which concludes the invention. The first
measure of this coda (22) has one more pair of en-
trances, in the treble on C, and in the bass on B.
The closing beats exploit right-side-up and upside-
down versions of the figure from beat four of measure
1.

Example 45.   Measures 20-23

CHAPTER 8: INVENTION NUMBER EIGHT (F MAJOR)

Canon is used to open this well-known piece, and the aural effect is somewhat more striking here than it is in Invention Two due to the absence of any well-delineated subject. This canon is strict at the lower octave until the second beat of measure 8, during which it becomes momentarily free, and then it continues for the better part of three more measures, at the seventh (lower ninth), concluding after the first beat of 11, just before the cadence at 11-12 which brings section one to a close. Sequence, as usual, plays an important role, dominating the treble passage at measures 4-6 with one-bar stages, and the ensuing passage at 8-10, with one-beat stages. Canonical procedure, of course, ensures sequential treatment in the imitating voice, and more than normal amounts of note-against-note (homorhythmic) activity exploiting parallel or similar motion result at certain locations, such as measures 5-6, because of this. The motive from measure 1, after its initial imitation, is kept alive intermittently throughout this section, each time with a different arrangement of scale degrees and intervals: at measures 3 and 4, on the tonic chord in F major, 7 on the dominant-seventh chord in C major, and 8 on the tonic chord in C. The bass response at the tonic in measure 8, to the treble at the dominant in 7, creates those changes in the interval of imitation which cause the canon to become free.

Example 46. Measures 1-12

Section two begins in the dominant key at measure 12, with the bass introducing what seems initially
as if it will be another canon--in invertible counterpoint with the opening canon, as happens in Invention
Two--but the bass pattern changes abruptly in conjunction with a chromatic modulation to G minor at 15, as
the treble ceases its imitation of the bass and brings
in a broken, or compound, melody. Measures 16-19 then
restate 12-15 in invertible counterpoint, except for
the treble part from 12, which has been supplanted by
material from 2 in the bass at 16. The same tonal relationships recur, as this second four-bar passage modulates from G minor to D minor in response to the earlier modulation from C to G, and the bass's broken melody at 19 then continues sequentially into 20, where
the treble has a varied statement of the opening motive
in D minor. Measure 21 provides a somewhat manipulated
version of the broken melody in the treble, and a freely inverted statement of the opening eighth-note motive in the bass, as the first stage of a sequence having second and third stages in measures 22 and 23, respectively, following which (at 24-25) the two voices
freely exchange material, touching upon F major as they
modulate to Bb major to prepare a return of the last
three-quarters of section one (Example 47).

Modulation into Bb major is essential to the struc
tural plan employed here, for the passage from measures 4-12, which began in the tonic key and modulated
up a fifth to the dominant, is brought back at 26-34,
starting in the subdominant key and modulating up a
fifth, to the tonic. The last nine measures of the
piece, therefore, result from transposition of the last

44   Chapter 8

Example 47. Measures 12-25

nine measures of section one, creating a somewhat rounded effect. The more traditional method of bringing off
a sense of return through restatement of the very opening materials is avoided here.

Example 48. Measures 26-34

CHAPTER 9:   INVENTION NUMBER NINE (F MINOR)

A fairly long subject is used as the basis for
the F-Minor Invention, only the Eb-Major Invention--a-
mong non-canonical inventions--having a generating i-
dea of greater length. Like the basic idea of Invention
Seven (and certain other odd-numbered inventions: E-
leven and Thirteen), the subject of Invention Nine begins on the fifth scale degree, as opposed to the more
conventional first scale degree (as in all the other
inventions), and it has a contour which rises sequentially in the second measure--although the sequence is
slightly clouded by a tie which connects the end of
stage one to the beginning of stage two--and non-se-
quentially to a high point during its third measure,
after which a winding-down process takes place. Accompaniment is provided by a countersubject, which be-
haves somewhat similarly, in terms of contour, until
the last half of measure 4, where it ascends, in contrary motion, to set up the bass presentation of the
subject.

Example 49.   Measures 1-5

The bass imitation of the treble subject, at the lower octave, is strict, as one would expect it to be. Imitation of the bass countersubject, which occurs in the treble, is also strict, while it lasts, starting a half beat late, in measure 5, and continuing for three measures, then becoming free in measure 8, as the bass is finishing the subject. The resulting invertible counterpoint has a three-octave interval of inversion.

Example 50. Measures 5-9

A three-bar version of the subject follows at measures 9-11, beginning still in F minor, and modulating to C minor. This version makes use of interval expansion into its third beat, where a rising tenth supplants what originally was a rising sixth, creating the transposition necessary for a continuation of the subject on its original scale degrees, but within the new key, which is a fifth higher. Octave displacement at the end of measure 10 provides additional variety and prevents the range from becoming excessively high. As this is occurring in the treble, the bass has the corresponding three-bar fragment of the countersubject, thus continuing the imitative process with the treble from measure 5, but likewise with octave displacement, after the first note. Its adjustment to the correct degrees for C minor occurs in the middle of 10, after it has become temporarily free. Measures 9-11 are then sequenced at 12-14, with octave displacement--the main alteration, other than transposition--causing restatement at both the lower fourth and upper fifth. Tonal movement by upward fifth, such as that observed with stage one of this sequence, with a modulation from F

minor to C minor, is manifested in stage two by a tonicization of the dominant chord in C minor (measures
13-14), and the upcoming cadence, at 16-17, although
harmonically imperfect, is strengthened considerably by
melodic and rhythmic means during 15 and 16, where the
treble hovers just below, on, and just above C, with
three two-beat units, which--during the two-bar pas-
sage--define C as the cadence point with great preci-
sion, creating the effect of hemiola (a rhythmic condition which frequently has cadential implications) as
they do. The bass, taking its material from the beginning of the third measure of the countersubject, is
temporarily sequential, with two-beat patterns (starting just after the first sixteenth of measure 15) which
reinforce the treble's hemiola.

Example 51.   Measures 9-17

The next section begins at measure 17, with a
statement of the subject (minus its first note) by the
bass, in the dominant minor key, accompanied by the
treble with the countersubject, which again becomes
free during its fourth measure (20), as a modulation
into Bb minor is set up. At 21-22, as the bass hints at
the countersubject and then becomes free, the treble
temporarily imitates at the fourth on different scale
degrees in Bb minor. The leap of a seventh into beat
three--the location where this subject has been previously manipulated--brings about a change in the interval of imitation and stifles the subject's second and
third bars, so that the treble--which, at measure 21
began imitating the bass from 17, at the fourth--con-
tinues at 22 by imitating the bass from measure *20*,

at the seventh. This treble imitation of the bass continues beyond the boundaries of the subject, into 23,
24, and part of 25; meanwhile, however, the bass, at
23-24, gets caught up with this new form of the subject
which unites its first and fourth bars while omitting
the second and third, and the result is invertible
counterpoint (23-24/21-22), within a new key, Ab major.

Example 52. Measures 17-24

A sequential passage ensues, with three stages in
the bass (25-26-27) on altered material from the first
measure of the countersubject, and two stages in the
treble (25-26) on altered material from the first measure of the subject. Both ideas start out transposed
within the relative major key, Ab major. The treble's
second beat is particularly interesting because of the
way it joins the original subject's second and third
beats, with rhythmic diminution and interval expansion.
Following a modulation back to F minor, through Db major, the bass at measure 28--doubled in tenths by the
treble after one beat--inverts itself from the immediately preceding sequential passage and prepares the
return (Example 53).

The subject returns intact at measures 29-32 in
the treble, accompanied by the countersubject in a varied form which is free during the first half of each
of the first two measures (29-30), but otherwise strict,
except for octave transposition and transposition of
its closing fragment at the lower third. Measure 33,
the penultimate measure, returns the melodic-rhythmic
cadential pattern from 16--but with internal transposi-

Example 53. Measures 25-28

tion in the treble--providing, along with the closing
measure, the only really conclusive-sounding cadence
of the piece.

Example 54. Measures 29-34

CHAPTER 10: INVENTION NUMBER TEN (G MAJOR)

A totally disjunct idea, which arpeggiates the G-major triad in such a way as to provide a high-note accent on the weakest portion of each beat, is used in the treble to get this invention under way, unaccompanied from the beginning (the last of the *Two-Part Inventions* to reflect this circumstance). The idea is more of a motive than a subject, and it is imitated in measure 2, *not* at the conventional octave, but rather at the fifth (lower eleventh), as in the earlier Eb-Major Invention. Although the motive, itself, has no feature which requires the use of a tonal answer, the bass does respond at the very end of measure 2, with imitation at the fourth (lower twelfth), thus contributing a seventh to the dominant chord, and doing its bit to prevent a modulation away from G major. The treble, meanwhile, inverts the first beat of the original motive, on the dominant chord, during the second and third beats of measure 2, with high-note accents contradicting those of the bass. There are no nonharmonic tones here, and, in fact, few throughout the piece because of the frequent employment of disjunct motion and note-against-note writing.

As the treble keeps arpeggiating in a descending fashion, using notes which tonicize the subdominant chord, the bass, in measure 3, continues its imitation of the treble (from measure 2), at the lower twelfth, beyond the point where the motive concludes, in a manner (reminiscent of the opening procedures in Inventions Four, Five, and Nine) which borders on canonical imitation, but never really becomes extensive, like the imitation in Inventions Two and Eight (Example 55).

Measure 4 establishes the first stage of a sequence in both voices, which still have arpeggiated chordal material on beats one and two, but virtually the first conjunct material of the piece on beat 3, in

53

Example 55. Measures 1-4

contrary motion. Descending second and third stages
appear at measures 5-6. Another sequence evolves at
measures 7-8, modulating to D major, and continuing
the descent, especially in the bass, which has now become almost totally conjunct, but also in the treble,
with the first note of each measure. The bass then,
in measure 9, imitates the treble from 8 (with an idea
which focuses mostly around an enlarged version of beat
two from the original motive), as the treble, in turn,
freely imitates the bass, creating a semblance of invertible counterpoint. At the beginning of measure 10,
a two-beat portion of this imitative treble thought is
sequenced as part of a larger, one-bar unit, which itself is treated somewhat sequentially, showing up in
transposition, with interval expansion, at 11 and 12.
The bass is strictly sequential starting with its moving eighths in measure 10. Contrary motion between the
two voices sets the stage for a solid cadence in D major, the only key other than G major which is well-
established in this piece.

Example 56. Measures 4-14

Section two begins at measure 14, in the new key, with the motive, typically enough, in the bass, unaccompanied after the first beat, and rounded off differently within 15 from the way it was in 2 (and 3), as the treble presents the tonal answer on the dominant-seventh chord in D major. A less typical procedure occurs at 16, as the bass presents its entry over again, but with the shape of a tonal answer modulating back to G major, rather than a subject. This latest bass entry is also imitated by the treble, now entirely at the fourth, with a tonicization of the subdominant chord at the end of measure 17. The second section's opening has a considerable amount of symmetry as a result of these back-and-forth entries and the invertible counterpoint they create.

Example 57. Measures 14-18

Sequence is called upon at measures 18-19--where the treble provides another metamorphosis of the opening idea, and the bass inverts a fragment from measure 7--and again at 20ff, where, as the treble holds a pedal, the bass takes over the immediately preceding treble

material, but with the first beat upside-down,¹ and restates it at the upper fourth (as opposed to the lower
second in the treble at 18-19). There are three stages
at 20-21-22 during which the treble's pedal drops one
degree, and another statement which breaks the pattern
of successive transpositions by rising fourth, in measure 23. The bass then acquires a pedal at 24-25, as
the treble becomes sequential with material based upon
fragments found earlier in the invention (for example,
in the bass during measure 7). At 26, the bass resumes
eighth-note activity, while the treble slows down its
note values in anticipation of the return.

Example 58. Measures 18-27

The original motive returns in the tonic key at
measure 27, presented by the treble, and answered tonally, *not* by the bass, as expected, but rather still by
the treble. Underlying both motive and answer, at 27-
28, are slightly embellished, transposed versions of
the treble line from measure 2--versions which create
free invertible counterpoint with that second measure.
As the bass limps sequentially part-way up the G-major
scale in measure 29, the treble sets up the scheme for

a cadence such as the one at 13-14, but an early ending at 30 is averted, when this cadence turns out to
be deceptive, initiating a short coda which extends
the piece briefly. The conjunct grouping on beats two
and three of measure 30, in the treble, is continued
sequentially into 31, where it is suffixed in such a
way as to become a restatement of measure-29 material
at the lower octave, after which this time the final
cadence opportunity is taken.

Example 59. Measures 27-32

CHAPTER 11:   INVENTION NUMBER ELEVEN (G MINOR)

An especially interesting approach to motivic de-
velopment can be observed in the G-Minor Invention,
which gets under way with a subject (beginning on the
fifth scale degree) built entirely out of sixteenth-
note fragments pieced together in different ways, during the first two measures. The second measure is completely derivative from the first, what with its first
two beats comprising the second stage of a falling sequence, begun during the last half of measure 1, and
beats three and four--in themselves sequential--relat-
ing back to beat two of measure 1, in inversion. The
bass is given a countersubject, which takes shape later than the subject and is characterized by more rhythmic variety, as well as an ornamented chromatic de-
scent--sequential in conjunction with the treble's se-
quence--until it concludes with a rising-fourth/fall-
ing-second tail motive, which is syncopated. The be-
havior of this countersubject throughout the piece is
about as important as that of the subject. In both
cases, motives are separated, redistributed, and otherwise manipulated, as the various passages unfold.

Example 60.   Measures 1-3

Octave imitation by the bass, beginning at measure 3, is momentarily doubled in tenths by the treble,
which has its presentation of the countersubject inverted, and also deferred, until the upbeat into 4, so

59

that only the sequential portion has time in which to appear. The tonic key is not well-pronounced with this entry, except at its beginning and ending, and this is a fairly unusual feature when imitation at the octave is involved. In fact, however, imitation is not found at the *perfect* octave throughout this entry, for alterations have been made within the third beat of measure 3 (F-natural) and first beat of 4 (Eb), to accommodate what seem to be tenuous references to other keys.

Example 61. Measures 3-5

The rest of this opening passage is given over to an episode (measures 5-6) in which the treble has a free two-stage sequence, based on the subject's first measure with a modified beginning. The bass starts moving with free eighth-note material after having continued its imitation of the treble into the first part of the episode, and a modulation through Bb major into D minor precedes an imperfect authentic cadence at 6-7.

Example 62. Measures 5-7

An ensuing D-minor bass statement of the subject (measures 7-8), accompanied by the treble, with the countersubject (again, as at the beginning, starting somewhat later than the subject) creates invertible counterpoint with the opening of the invention, and it is this feature, more than any concluding feature brought on by a cadence, which suggests the beginning of a new section. In the absence of imitation at mea-

sures 9-10, however, this area becomes episodic somewhat earlier than before. It exploits enlarged versions of the countersubject's tail motive by the treble
(measure 9) in counterpoint with half-bar sequential
groupings of the subject's second beat, first inverted
(as a sequential continuation of the subject's tail)
and then uninverted. A retrograde-inversion of the same
four-note configuration (beat one of measure 10 in the
bass) is followed by sequential references to the subject's opening four notes, and then a cadence (measures 10-11), which, like the previous one, is authentic, in D minor, but perfect rather than imperfect.

Example 63. Measures 7-11

The episode continues then through the cadence
and on into the beginning of the next passage, which
illustrates an ingenious method for associating over-
lapping fragments of the subject contrapuntally, as
material comprising the subject's *first* two beats shows
up in the bass on the *second* and *third* beats of measure
11, along with material from its second, third, and
fourth beats, on beats two, three, and four, in the
treble. A key change, through F major into C minor,
helps to propel the passage onward into measure 12,
where the bass imitates the treble from 11--but with
a change in the interval of imitation between beats
one and two--and the treble devotes itself to sequential thoughts which anticipate a full statement of the
subject during the following two measures.

This treble statement (13-14), in the subdominant
minor key, is accompanied by the same material in the

bass, that the bass statement of measures 3-4 was accompanied by in the treble, and the result is invertible counterpoint between the two pairs of measures, although the interval of inversion changes on the third beat of measure 13 because of octave displacement by the bass. Measures 15-16 have double-octave imitation of the subject, in the bass, but this imitation is not complete, breaking off as it does after the first beat of 16, just prior to the perfect authentic cadence which concludes this section. Instead of employing the countersubject along with this incomplete bass entry, the treble, at measure 15, restates the bass material from 13, in part, producing invertible counterpoint once again.

Example 64. Measures 11-16

The final section begins transitionally, in the middle of measure 16, with a sequential statement of two stages, by the bass, on the first measure of the subject, which modulates into Eb major, but on scale degrees within the key which are different from the original ones. This material is virtually identical with the treble material in measures 5-6, but here the first two notes of the subject are included in the initial stage, and there they were not. Resemblance between the two passages is not confined to these two measures, for the bass from the fourth beat of 16 to the middle of 21 is strict with the treble from the second beat of 5 to the beginning of 10 at the lower perfect twelfth. The treble does not follow suit here by duplicating the earlier bass part, until the middle of measure 18, after a modulation back to the tonic key has taken place. Then, it returns the entire subject, in G minor, creating invertible counterpoint with the parallel location in the earlier passage, at measures 7-8, as well as recalling the invention's opening. The sequential continuation in the treble during the last half of measure 20 carries this invertible counterpoint even further, by identifying back to the bass part at the beginning of measure 9. In effect, then, this return, which starts in the middle of measure 18, corroborates the passage starting at the beginning of 7, in terms of materials and the way they are used, to a greater extent than it corroborates the opening of the piece, although it does, of course, use the tonality from the opening.

Example 65.   Measures 16-21

The final three measures of the piece utilize i-solated fragments of the subject and countersubject distributed in various manners. The subject's scale-wise beginning is found right-side-up in the treble at the beginning of measure 21, and upside-down in the bass, at the end. Its second beat appears in retro-grade-inversion on the third beat of measure 21, and in inversion, on the second and fourth beats of 22, all in the treble. The countersubject's tail motive appears with interval expansion in the bass at the be-ginning of 21 (duplicating the treble from the end of 9), and in its original form, at the end of 22. The subject's fourth beat is used, with interval contrac-tion, as the final melodic idea of the piece (measure

23, beat two).

Example 66. Measures 21-23

CHAPTER 12: INVENTION NUMBER TWELVE (A MAJOR)

The form of Invention Twelve brings to mind that
of Invention Five, because the sections of these two
works (which have approximately the same proportional
length in terms of the overall length of the work) are
defined more by contrapuntal, than by cadential means,
and because each of the two has a subject which is imitated at the fifth, a factor which perhaps influenced
the key choice for the beginning of section two: the
relative minor, in both instances; in fact, the first
few key relationships of Invention Twelve (A major, E
major, A major, and F-sharp minor) parallel those of
Invention Five (Eb major, Bb major, Eb major, and C
minor) at the tritone. Another similarity between the
two involves modulation within the framework of the
subject, and the tonal nature of the responding bass
imitation.

The A-Major Invention opens with a subject, the
precise extent of which is open to interpretation. Because of the "afterthought" character of the treble
material at the end of measure 2, the subject could be
construed as ending on the beginning of beat three and
being followed by a link; however, links are notably
rare between first and second entries in Bach's *Inventions* and *Fugues*, and because this particular half-bar
appendage is found as part of each and every statement
of the subject and answer, except the very final one--
where its omission avoids a modulation away from the
tonic key, allowing for the piece to end gracefully,
soon after its completion--it would seem appropriate
for one to consider it an intrinsic part of the subject. The modulation into the dominant key brought a-
bout by this half-measure segment creates the neces-
sity for a tonal adjustment in the subsequent answer.

A countersubject is presented by the bass in measures 1-2, its initial head portion relating to a tail

65

portion (beat one of measure 2) from the subject, itself, through melodic inversion. The second beat of the countersubject sequences the first, at the lower third, and the fourth beat sequences the third, in the same fashion. The countersubject then changes character, switching from sixteenth-notes to eighths, before dropping out entirely, at the end of measure 2.

Example 67. Measures 1-3

The bass, at measure 3, begins imitating at the fifth (lower eleventh), and changes--in a manner typical of the reply to a modulating subject--to the fourth (lower twelfth) for its closing fragment (the last seven sixteenth-notes of measure 4, as they lead into 5). This tonal adjustment, of course, is necessary to prevent a modulation into the supertonic key, and to reconcile the answer's ending in the tonic key, with the subject's ending in the dominant. The countersubject, meanwhile, appears in the treble, becoming strict after the first two sixteenths of measure 3 (thus creating invertible counterpoint with the beginning), then freeing itself on the second beat of measure 4, after which the treble line continues beyond the point corresponding to that where the bass originally ended (Example 68).

Measures 5-8 are episodic in nature, although the treble, in measure 5, begins as if to present an additional (redundant) opening entry, and, in fact, this measure does give the impression of containing a telescoped subject--having the first two beats of the head motive followed by the end of the tail, freely inverted and then repeated. The bass features the countersub-

Example 68. Measures 3-5

3

4

ject somewhat similarly. Measure 6 starts out to sequence measure 5, in both voices, down one degree, but
becomes free during its second half, which employs, a-
mong other things, interval expansion and contraction.
The next two measures (7-8) focus on a variant of beat
three from measure 2, combining its individual statements into one continuous line, within a texture which
is virtually monophonic for several beats. The upper
voice here continues the motivic pattern of the lower
voice at the upper fourth, in half-bar groupings which
descend sequentially by second, creating fairly extensive root movement by falling fifth, and modulating
into the relative minor key. The dominant-seventh/ton-
ic progression at the end of measure 8 and beginning
of 9 does not create much effect of cadence, because
of its high degree of imperfection, and the close of
section one is determined as much by what is obviously
the beginning of section two, as it is by any cadential procedure.

Example 69. Measures 5-9

5

Invention Number Twelve   67

Section two begins in F-sharp minor (the relative minor, rather than the more customary dominant, found with most major-key, and some minor-key inventions), with a subject statement which has an embellished head portion, followed by an unembellished tail. Because the subject's initial entry has been positioned in the treble (as in Invention Seven at the corresponding location), rather than the more traditional bass, there is no role reversal for the two voices, here, in relationship to what they did at the beginning. However, architectural similarities which often relate section two to section one, in conjunction with the voice exchange provided by invertible counterpoint, are manifested here without it, for the nine-bar passage from 9 to 18 tends to duplicate the seven-and-one-half-bar passage from 1 to the middle of 8, in transposition (at more than one level) except for a one-and-one-half-measure insertion during 13 and the first half of 14 (an insertion which is reminiscent of a similar passage in the second section of Invention One).

The treble's account of the subject at measures 9-10 is accompanied by the countersubject in the bass, which provides another new twist at the end of 10, the location analogous to that in which the bass was resting during measure 2. The subject modulates from F-sharp minor to *its* dominant, C-sharp minor, setting up imitation at the fifth (lower eleventh) by the bass, in measures 11-12. This imitation of the subject in the bass is accompanied by imitation of the counter-subject in the treble, and once again, the countersubject becomes free--in yet another way--during its second measure (12). The answer is tonal, like its predecessor in measures 3-4, but its very ending has been altered in such a way as to set up a modulation which does not lead back to F-sharp minor, but rather into B minor, temporarily, prior to the return of the tonic key, shortly thereafter. The last half-bar segment of the answer's tail, in the bass at the end of measure 12, becomes the point-of-departure for a sequence having four stages which are strict (in terms of their intervals' numerical size) except for octave displacement that affects the third and fourth stages. These two-beat thoughts are accompanied in the treble by tri-partite patterns of repetition which create the effect of hemiola during the last half of measure 12, throughout measure 13, and on into 14. This rhythmic feature thus begins before the answer is completed and persists throughout the one-and-one-half-bar passage during 13 and the first part of 14, which intrudes upon this section's structural duplication of section one-- a passage which contributes tonal variety and prepares the tonic key.

Example 70. Measures 9-14

11

12

13   14

The middle of measure 14, then, brings back the
beginning of 5, down a fifth in the treble, and at the
original pitch level in the bass. Freedoms are taken
at the beginning of 15 (in relation to the end of 5),
but from the middle of 15 through 17, measures 6, 7,
and the first half of 8 are brought back, down a fifth
in the treble, and first up a fourth, then down a fifth
in the bass. The premature entrance of the subject
(by two beats) in the bass at the beginning of measure
18 brings the correspondence between sections two and
one to an end, but not before even more extensive root
movement by descending fifth than that found previous-
ly--involving all degrees of the diatonic scale on A--
has unfolded, this time without any modulation (Example 71).

The final appearance of the subject is an incomplete appearance in the bass at measures 18-19, accompanied by the treble, which initially provides balance by presenting a portion of that material from the
subject's tail (beat three of the second measure) which
is omitted by the bass at the end of 19, where the
third beat sequences the second beat, and so does the
fourth, thus averting the modulation which has been a

Example 71. Measures 14-18

normal feature of the subject. This entry is not accompanied by the countersubject, as such, but a countersubject fragment (from beats three and four) does
appear on the third and fourth beats of measure 18, in
the treble, and the countersubject's eighth-note rhythm
abounds in measure 19. An answer at the subdominant,
metrically displaced by one beat and still in the bass
voice, is suggested within measure 20, but it fails to
materialize, as an altered version of the subject's
ending appears in the treble, lending another brief
moment of balance. The material of measure 21 is free,
but derivative, and the final cadence makes use of an
unusual feminine ending (Example 72).

Example 72. Measures 18-21

CHAPTER 13: INVENTION NUMBER THIRTEEN (A MINOR)

The A-Minor Invention is unique among the *Two-Part Inventions* in that it emphasizes materials which relate to the generating idea (and its sequel), found during measure 1, in a manner which is more rhythmic than it is melodic. This opening idea is a sixteenth-note motive found in the treble (starting on the fifth scale degree) during the first half of measure 1 and imitated by the bass during the second half, following which--in measure 2--it is restated, in the manner of Invention Four, and re-imitated, in the manner of Inventions One and Seven, but without transposition (inventions based on motives favor this repetitive feature to a greater degree than do those based on subjects). The eighth-note bass line in the first half of measure 2 provides what might be termed a countermotive, since it shows up again during the first half of 7, and twice in 18, in counterpoint with the sixteenth-note motive, but the treble line in the last half of measure 1 is recycled in a similar manner during the last half of 7, and all of the motivic ideas from the first two measures are, in fact, used less pervasively than are some of the materials which derive from them. Widespread use of arpeggiated chords--here and throughout the invention--results in the employment of a minimal number of nonharmonic tones (as in Invention Ten).

Example 73.   Measures 1-3

Measures 3-6 provide a modulatory episode based on material which starts out, in the treble, by duplicating time values but not pitches from the treble in measure 1. This material comes about as close as any in the *Two-Part Inventions* to being new material, and after it has been given out by the treble, it is imitated at the fourth (lower twelfth) by the bass. Since not just the falling disjunct sixteenth-note line, but the rising eighth-note line as well, is included in the imitation, a canonical effect results, especially when--as the passage modulates into the relative major key--the treble in measure 4 sequences itself from 3, and the bass at least starts to follow suit. Two-way imitation within this chain of events produces a brief area of invertible counterpoint (between the first half of 4 and the last half of 3, etc.). The episode then continues sequentially (measures 5-6) with three half-bar stages, which provide a compressed version of the previous one-bar stages in the treble and two similarly compressed and otherwise modified bass stages which help set up the C-major cadence ending section one.

Example 74. Measures 3-6

The second section begins with the bass presenting a C-major version of the invention's opening motive, followed, in measure 7, by the treble with imitation at the upper octave, in the traditional manner; however, after its sixteenth-note motive is out, the treble continues just as it did during measure 1, with eighth-note material different from that of the bass, which also keeps *its* original line going, so that measure 7 contains the treble material from measure 1 in counterpoint with the bass material from 2, all in

transposition up a third. The treble keeps this process of restatement alive during most of measure 8, and
so does the bass, following its rests, where a new level of transposition is employed for the beginning of a
new episode. Insofar as the sixteenth-note motive it-
self· is concerned, then, the opening two measures of
the piece have been brought back with the two voice-
parts exchanged, from the middle of measure 6 to the
middle of 8, although invertible counterpoint, a device which is found at the beginning of the second section in many inventions, is not provided by the accompanying material to any great extent.

Example 75. Measures 6-8

        The ensuing episode, which modulates quite prompt-
ly into G major, maintains many similarities with its
counterpart at the beginning of measure 3 and after--
similarities which are quite apparent within the con-
text of voice exchange despite the employment of certain modifying devices such as interval contraction and
expansion, which prohibit all but a very free sense of
canon, in contrast to the brief but stricter canon
found within the earlier episode.

        An additional one-bar pattern, from the middle of
measure 10 to the middle of 11, causes this latter episode to part company with the earlier one, but the
paralleling process resumes--at least in the treble--
on the last beat of measure 11, where the two voices
are re-reversed, as the treble pattern from the first
beat of measure 5 is brought back, transposed up a
third, with a not-too-commonly seen type of metrical
displacement from strong beat to weak, so that all
four beats of measure 5 along with the first beat of
measure 6 return .during the passage beginning with the
last beat of 11 and continuing through all four beats
of 12. The bass--sequential like the treble--employs a
more active version of the same material one beat in
advance, so in effect the treble is imitating the bass

Invention Number Thirteen 75

skeletally, while it is returning this earlier passage. The sequence dissolves just before material modulating to the dominant minor key contributes the one-beat extension which is necessary for a cadence on the strong beat in the middle of measure 13. This cadence, a perfect authentic cadence in E minor, is somewhat analogous to the one in the middle of measure 6, and it does fulfill the function of closing section two, as the earlier cadence closed section one, but it is spun out through the measure, so that the next section's beginning does not elide with this section's ending, a condition which, along with the previously observed extending feature, contributes to the greater length of section two over section one.

Example 76. Measures 8-13

The opening of section three, at measure 14, is marked by further metamorphosis of the sixteenth-note derivative motive from measure 3, with its first beat inverted, its second beat uninverted (but characterized by interval contraction), and third and fourth beats--outlining harmony which is quite similar to that outlined on beats one and two--tacked on. This idea (all in sixteenth-notes) starts out in the treble and then migrates to the bass, as the first one-measure

stage of a four-stage sequence, which suggests a different key (outlined, for the most part, by the diminished seventh chord on the leading-tone, followed by
the dominant seventh chord) in each measure: D minor
in measure 14; C major (with borrowed-chord material)
in 15; E minor (on different scale degrees within the
key) in 16; and A minor in 17, by which point a return
of the opening has been set up. During the course of
this four-measure passage, both voices are sequential,
although measure 16 has subtle changes which keep the
sequence strict (in terms of the numerical size of its
intervals) from an enharmonic standpoint, while adjust-
ing the notes to conform to E minor (a closely related
key), rather than Bb (the key which would have fit in
with the modulatory scheme of tonalities falling by
degree). Because the three different diminished seventh chords which compositely account for all twelve
tones are employed so prominently here, one even ap-
pearing in two different enharmonic forms (B D F Ab in
measure 15, and G-sharp B D F in 17), the passage has
a high degree of instability.

Example 77. Measures 14-18

The return, at measure 18, resolves pent-up harmonic tension, which has been generated by the preceding passage, without benefit of a strong cadence,
so that it sounds integral to the section which is al-
ready in progress (a common circumstance in the *Two-
Part Inventions*). It brings back the passage from the
first half of measure 2 of the piece, however, rather

than measure 1, presenting the second half of the measure in invertible counterpoint with the first half, and then continuing, at measure 19, with an episodic passage which takes its cue *not* from the events of measure 3, as might be expected, but instead from those of measure 14, particularly in the treble, which begins by transposing the treble part from 14, at the lower fifth, as well as the sixteenth-note portion of the bass part from the same location, at the upper fourth. The bass has a less strict account of a half-bar treble fragment from 14, and it regroups in the middle of 19, then reverts to eighth-notes in 20 and 21, as the treble keeps its entire one-bar thought alive, in transposition, with various melodic distortions. This passage is strung out into measure 22.

Example 78. Measures 18-22

At the middle of measure 22, the original motive of the invention, found in the treble, initiates a coda-like passage characterized initially by a summing-up sequence which evolves at 23 with one-beat stages in both voices. Mixture of the three minor scale forms and the use of a Neapolitan-sixth chord (measure 23, beat four) create some of the more colorful harmonies of the piece, as the harmonic rhythm quickens during the course of this passage. Harmonic interest is sustained into the final two measures (24-25), as melodic materials become further liberated from their original sources (Example 79).

Example 79. Measures 22-25

CHAPTER 14: INVENTION NUMBER FOURTEEN (Bb MAJOR)

The Bb-Major Invention is architecturally distinctive in that it has what is indisputably a link between the first two entries. The opening exposition consists of a treble subject, accompanied by a bass countersubject (measures 1-4), a link (4-5), and then a bass answer, accompanied by a treble countersubject (6-9). These subject/answer entries are the only completely strict entries of the entire piece, but the usual economy of material has still been achieved, because important motivic ideas throughout, relate back to what happens during the first half of measure 1.

The subject, like the piece, itself, is highly economical. Its three measures have six statements of just one rhythmic pattern--an energetic, attention-capturing pattern which exploits thirty-second and sixteenth notes in half-bar units--used in conjunction with free melodic inversion (within each of the first two measures), and free sequence (between measures 1 and 2). Measure 3 does away with inversion, but keeps the sequential feature alive, with half-bar, rather than whole-bar stages. The countersubject, by way of contrast, is relatively inactive, accomplishing little more than an outlining of the harmonies implicit within each measure of the subject, essentially the primary triads: tonic, subdominant, and dominant, in slower-moving time values (Example 80).

The link, in measures 4-5, has a double sequence on the subject's first six notes, right-side-up in the bass (but with a rising fourth, rather than a rising fifth into the second beat), alternating with an upside-down version in the treble, in such a way that the texture is largely monophonic. Both voices start out to be sequential with half-bar stages, but become compressed and change their intervals of restatement, after measure 5 gets under way (Example 81).

81

Example 80. Measures 1-4

Example 81. Measures 4-6

A real answer, in the dominant major key, is then given out by the bass, which is strict with the treble from the beginning at the fifth (lower eleventh). For the first two measures (6-7), the original bass countersubject shows up in the treble at the upper twelfth, creating invertible counterpoint at the triple octave, but the countersubject becomes free during measure 8, where it retains only its general shape from before (Example 82).

Example 82. Measures 6-9

An episodic passage begins in measure 9, where the treble presents the subject's first half-bar segment at the lower perfect fourth, followed by the subsequent half-bar segment, mostly (but not completely) at the lower second, while the bass has continuous-sounding countersubject material without the original rests, in free inversion. This episode is modulatory in nature, moving into G minor during the first measure (9), Eb-major during the second (10), where the two voices imitate each other from the previous measure in such a way as to create free invertible counterpoint, and C minor during the third (11), where the voices re-exchange, to resume their original order from measure 9 (Example 83).

Still another modulation--this one back to the tonic key of the invention--takes place in measure 12, where still new treatment is applied to the subject's opening fragment. Here, it shows up with the original rising fifth into beat two enlarged to an octave, the upper note of which descends conjunctly, using dotted-note rhythm, as the first half-bar stage of a sequence which has three more stages, ascending by fourth, all

Invention Number Fourteen 83

Example 83. Measures 9-12

in the bass. The same material, presented by the treble but deferred by one beat, creates a short canon at the double octave, which lasts until the fourth beat of measure 13, where the treble momentarily imitates in inversion, setting off a long passage in which the two voices appear homorhythmically, doubled in tenths, first with sequence on the opening six-note fragment of the subject in inversion (during the first part of 14), then with longer, half-bar stages (four in all), which alternate similar forms of the same fragment, right-side-up, and in inversion, from the middle of 14 to the middle of 16 (Example 84).

After this passage (which is one of the *Two-Part Inventions'* longest note-against-note passages in parallel motion) concludes, the bass brings about a return by announcing, in the tonic key, close to two-thirds of the original subject, strictly, and the remaining portion--plus an extension--freely, its third measure (from the middle of 18 to the middle of 19) retaining the upside-down feature found with its first

Example 84. Measures 12-16

two measures, but not measure 3, originally. The treble, meanwhile, starting on the last beat of 16, provides octave imitation, which, because of the length of the subject and the closeness of the time interval (one beat), produces a canonical effect once again. This imitation becomes temporarily free on the third beat of 17, but resumes on the fourth beat strictly, continuing until the middle of 18, where it concludes entirely, although the treble, like the bass, continues to spin out material from the subject into measure 19, where, on beat three, just before the final cadential pattern, the two voices converge with inverted and uninverted statements of the ubiquitous opening fragment.

Invention Number Fourteen 85

Example 85.   Measures 16-20

CHAPTER 15:   INVENTION NUMBER FIFTEEN (B MINOR)

Like four of the earlier inventions (Numbers Five, Ten, Twelve, and Fourteen), Invention Fifteen employs imitation at the fifth, rather than the octave, during its opening exposition. The treble subject ends at the beginning of measure 3, and like many of Bach's subjects, it has a high degree of internal unity, here in the form of recurrent figures, modified by means of transposition, interval expansion, etc. It is accompanied by the incipient form of a countersubject, which is situated--in a more active version--with each entry of the subject or answer, throughout the invention. A Phrygian cadence facilitates the modulation into F-sharp minor for the answer.

Example 86. Measures 1-3

This answer is essentially a real answer in the dominant minor key, but one having distilled imitation in the bass on the fourth beat of measure 4 (in relation to the treble material on the fourth beat of measure 2), a change which is only the first of several changes taking place at the endings of subject and answer entries throughout the piece. The countersubject is treated similarly, but with alterations occurring about as often during its beginning portion, as its ending. Freedom near the end of the countersubject is exhibited as early as the last half of measure 4, where

embellished imitation of the bass by the treble, at
the fifth, which began in measure 3 (the first note of
each beat jibing with the one-note-per-beat of the bass
in measures 1-2) becomes free, somewhat in conjunction
with the freedom of the answer in relation to the subject. Although the countersubject, as it is found in
measures 3-4, takes its overall shape from the sparsely
stated eighth notes in the bass during measures 1 and
2, it also relates to the subject's sixteenth-note tail
portion, which through its subdivision of the beat anticipates and defines the prevailing character of all
subsequent countersubject appearances. The ending of
the answer coincides with the *beginning* of a cadential
pattern, rather than the ending (as with the subject),
for it delineates an implied cadential six-four chord
which helps establish a strikingly conclusive-sounding
cadence for so early in the piece--a perfect authentic
cadence in F-sharp minor, strengthened by an anticipa-
tion--in the middle of measure 5.

Example 87.   Measures 3-5

   The subject is then brought back by the treble,
in the dominant minor key, with its ending (beats two
and three of measure 7) reshaped, in a manner different from that of the answer. The bass countersubject
which accompanies this entry helps create invertible
counterpoint between this passage (from the middle of
5 to the middle of 7) and the previous passage at measures 3-4, first ornamentally, and then strictly; it
concludes, however, by modifying the earlier treble
configuration on which it is based (from the last half

of 4) in such a way that it generates a false entry at the beginning of measure 7. During the second half of 7, then, this false entry is imitated by the treble, as the closing configuration of the subject from the beginning of the measure is imitated by the bass, so that more invertible counterpoint results (at the twelfth, compounded by an octave), all within measure 7.

Example 88. Measures 5-7

This invertible counterpoint marks the beginning of an episode which modulates almost immediately back to B minor, but only as a temporary tonal diversion on its way to the next important key, the relative major. Its principal derivative material--on the odd-numbered treble beats of measures 8-9, and throughout 10, as well as during the first half of 11 in the bass--comes from the third beat of the countersubject, as found originally on beat three of measure 3, in the treble. The disjunct treble material on the even beats of 8-9, on the other hand, seems to relate more to the subject. Sequence plays an important role here, strictly in the bass--which has one-bar stages in evenly moving eighth notes, with the second group of four notes within each stage inverting the first--and freely in the treble, which has both half-bar and one-bar stages at the same time. In measure 10, the treble remains sequential, having one-beat stages on the motive from the third beat of measure 3, but with interval expansion into the fourth note of each beat, throughout most of the measure. The bass acquisition of this motive in measure 11 is without any such enlargement, although it too is sequential, as the treble supplies the subject's rhythm, with mostly different melodic configurations, which make it, in turn, sequential again. The section is completed at the start of measure 12, in D major.

Example 89. Measures 7-12

The new section functions in much the same way that section *two* functions in other minor-key inventions, having first a bass statement of the subject in the relative major key (measures 12-14) followed by a treble statement, which answers the subject with imitation at the fifth, in A major (14-16). This subject has a shape which is closer to the shape of the original subject than is that of any other entry in the piece, although it does--unlike the first entry--modulate up a fifth to set up the answer. Both entries are accompanied by countersubject material--the first for about six beats (with octave displacement at the very beginning of measure 12), and the second, for a shorter time, since freedoms are taken at both start and finish.

Example 90. Measures 12-16

A transitory modulation into E minor takes place during the answer's ending, which, along with its accompanying eighth-note counterpoint, contributes material for the ensuing episode. Here (measures 15-17), the bass has an idea like that occurring in measures 8-9, but without any inversion, and with half-bar sequential stages (the third of which is displaced downward two octaves), rather than whole-bar stages as before, while the treble capitalizes on another modified version of the answer's tail. Throughout this brief episode, both voices are sequential, with stages which initially ascend by fifth (or descend by fourth, as the case may be) along with changes in the tonality by the same interval, from E minor to B minor, and then to F-sharp minor. Two further key changes, to E minor and D major then accommodate an idea having the subject's opening rhythm but different pitches, forming a two-beat unit which is then sequenced at the lower ninth, in the bass at 17-18, in counterpoint with a sequential continuation of the treble thought from 16 in a slightly new form, with octave displacement at the end of the first four-note group (of 17) and change-of-direction into the second.

Example 91. Measures 15-18

The tonic key returns along with the subject, in measure 18, as the treble continues in a freely sequential manner, then slips into the countersubject on the third beat. This countersubject presentation remains strict only for a short time, however, then is broken off, just before the treble introduces the subject in

Invention Number Fifteen   91

premature imitation of the bass, creating a very loose stretto effect, even though the subject's ending in the bass is convoluted into the countersubject, starting with the last two notes of measure 19. The treble imitation occurs at the octave, and it becomes free in still a different way--in keeping with what has been a practice throughout this invention--within measure 21, just after the bass has brought in a variant of the subject's head-motive. A brief moment in which the bass (on beat 3) imitates the treble (from beat 2) prefaces the final cadence of the piece.

Example 92. Measures 18-22

79; Number 14 (Bb Major),
81-86, 87; Number 15 (B
Minor), 87-92

Voice crossing, *see e.g.*
Examples 12 (m. 18), 51
(m. 12), 69 (mm. 7 and
8), 71 (mm. 16 and 17),
90 (m. 13)

Made in the USA
Las Vegas, NV
03 September 2021